Dexter Informa's Interesting Facts About Nature

For Smart Kids, Curious Adults and Trivia Hunters!

Dexter Informa

Dexter Informa

Dexter Informa is on his travels exploring the world for more interesting facts to excite and amaze!

If you would like to know when the next book is available then follow the link below and sign up to find out more!

bit.ly/dexter-informa

Table of Contents

Introduction: The Wonder and Marvels of Nature

In all its small details and vast beauty, nature hides secrets that have been puzzling people for thousands of years. Our planet is full of things that surprise and fascinate us, like the echoing chambers of mysterious underwater caves and the strange mating dances of forest-dwelling birds. Yet, in our efforts to understand how big the universe is or how complicated we are, we often miss the simple, fun facts that our natural world has to offer.

Welcome to a trip that shows off these amazing things. This book is not just a list of facts; it is also a tribute to the strange things about Earth. Trivia is fun because it can surprise us with just a few words and remind us that there is always something new to learn, even about things we thought we knew a lot about. Did you know that there is a plant that can "remember" and a bacterium that eats metal? Even though these bits of information might not seem like much, they can lead to bigger questions and thoughts about the world.

This book is set up to take you through different habitats and natural events, from the depths of the ocean to the vastness of our deserts. Each section shows how Earth can always surprise us. We learn about the science and stories behind plants, animals, climates, and geographical wonders as we explore their world.

Even though the focus is on fun and interesting facts, there is also a subtle reminder that our planet, with all its quirks, is valuable. The more we learn about it and are amazed by it, the more we realize how important it is to care for and protect it.

So, turn the page and start this fun adventure of learning. Let us celebrate the wonders of Earth's nature together, whether you read one fact a day or the whole book at once.

-   *Dexter Informa*

Marine and Ocean Life

- The Great Barrier Reef, the largest living structure on Earth with a length of over 2,300 kilometers, can be seen from space.

- Oceans hold about 96.5% of Earth's water and make up about 71% of its surface.

- The world's oceans have only been explored to a degree of about 5% and mapped to a degree of less than 26%

- With a surface area of more than 30%, the Pacific Ocean is the largest ocean in the world.

- With a depth of 36,201 feet, the Mariana Trench is the deepest area of the oceans in the entire world.

- Often referred to as "rainforests of the sea," coral reefs are the ecosystem of 25% of marine species.

- The deepest parts of the ocean are cold and completely dark because of high pressures.

- Global temperatures are regulated by the Great Ocean Conveyor Belt, a network of ocean currents.

- About 25% of all the carbon dioxide produced is absorbed by the oceans, reducing the effects of global warming.

- The heart of the Blue Whale, the biggest animal on Earth, is the size of a small car.

- The majority of the oxygen on Earth is produced by phytoplankton, tiny marine plants.

- The sea cucumber can regenerate its internal organs after expelling them to frighten away potential predators.

- After maturing, the Immortal Jellyfish has the ability to go back to its baby state.

- Deep-sea creatures frequently exhibit bioluminescence, a phenomenon in which living things emit light as a result of a chemical reaction.

- Coral is made up of tiny creatures called polyps; it is not a plant.

- The only animal species in which the male goes through pregnancy and childbirth is the seahorse and their close relative, the sea dragon.

- Mountains, valleys, and vast plains can be found in the deepest parts of the ocean.

- Because starfish lack brains, they navigate using a network of nerves.

- To avoid predators, the mimic octopus can assume the appearance of other animals.

- One of the most sophisticated systems of vision ever discovered is found in mantis shrimp.

- In the North Pacific Ocean, there is a persistent "garbage patch" that is primarily made up of plastic waste.

- A land-dwelling ancestor that existed about 50 million years ago gave rise to whales.

- Long tusks on narwhals are actually teeth that can get as long as 10 feet long.

- At the bottom of the ocean, there is a pressure of more than eight tons per square inch, which is the same as 50 jumbo jets being held by one person.

- Manatee relatives known as dugongs graze on aquatic grasses day and night, snuffling and chomping them with their rough lips and bristled, sensitive snouts.

- A species of deep-sea sponge called the Harp Sponge uses long spines that resemble Velcro to catch prey.

- Because of the way its gills resemble Christmas trees, the "Christmas tree worm" received its name.

- The Black Dragonfish has teeth that are virtually invisible due to their extreme transparency.

- The goblin shark of the deep sea can extend its jaws to capture prey.

- When the dominant female dies, clownfish, made famous by the movie "Finding Nemo," switch to the opposite sex.

- The Pistol Shrimp can close its claw so quickly that a bubble reaching a temperature of over 8000 °F is produced, making a small implosive sound.

- Small islands and sandy beaches have been created by parrotfish, which consume coral and excrete sand.

- The world's most venomous fish is the stonefish.

- The most venous marine animal is thought to be the box jellyfish, which is found in Australian waters.

- "Lakes" and "rivers" exist in the ocean. The bodies of water in these brine pools are much saltier than the ocean outside.

- An octopus has three hearts: two of them supply the gills with blood, and the third one supplies the rest of the body.

- Many more islands than can be found in all of Earth's other oceans can be found in the Pacific Ocean, which has about 25,000 different types.

- Up to 50 gallons of water can be filtered by oysters each day.

- Triggerfish can swim backwards.

- Using its wing-like fins, the Flying Fish can float through the air for up to 200 meters.

- The tentacles of the lion's mane jellyfish can reach up to 120 feet.

- When illuminated, the Halitrephes jellyfish resembles a fireworks display.

- Underwater hot springs called hydrothermal vents spew out water that is rich in minerals.

- The absence of erythrocytes and haemoglobin accounts for the clear blood of Antarctic Icefish.

- Because of where their eyes are located on their distinctively shaped heads, hammerhead sharks can see 360 degrees around them.

- Some Greenland Sharks are thought to be more than 400 years old, making them some of the oldest living vertebrates.

- The deep-sea fangtooth fish is only a few inches long, despite its intimidating appearance and long fangs.

- Depending on the best gender for mating, oysters can change their gender.

- Sharks can detect electric fields thanks to a sixth sense they have called electroreception.

- Oceanic tides on Earth are greatly influenced by the moon.

- A pufferfish's toxin is 1,200 times more lethal than cyanide.

- Climate change is causing an increase in "ocean deserts," regions of the ocean with few nutrients and little life.

- To draw prey in the deep sea, female anglerfish have a bioluminescent lure on their heads.

Flora's Fascinations

- On Earth, there are over 390,000 different species of plants.

- In one day, bamboo can reach a height of 91 cm.

- 20% of the oxygen consumed worldwide is produced in the Amazon rainforest.

- Freshly cut grass has a distinct aroma that serves as a plant's distress signal. What you can smell is a chemical that distressed plants release.

- Acorns are not produced by oak trees until they are 50 years or older.

- There is a type of orchid that strikingly resembles a monkey's face.

- The cacao tree, which provides us with chocolate, has a 200-year lifespan. But only for the first 25 years of its life does it produce beans.

- The Titan Arum plant only blooms for one day every 40 years.

- More than 80,000 different plant species are edible.

- Radioactive waste can be cleaned up by sunflowers. After the Chernobyl accident, they were used to remove radioactive cesium from the nearby ponds.

- Using chemicals and underground fungi networks, trees can "communicate" with one another.

- Memory can be enhanced by the aroma of rosemary.

- The Old English word "plante," which means a young tree or herb, is where the word "plant" originates.

- Some plants, such as the Venus flytrap, are insect-eating carnivores.

- Vanilla flavoring is extracted from the pod of the Vanilla planifolia orchid.

- A plant known as the "resurrection plant" can go for months without water and will come back to life in a matter of hours after being hydrated.

- The same plant species is the source of Brussels sprouts, cabbage, cauliflower, and broccoli.

- An African baobab tree with a bar inside was discovered in 1987. It was wide enough to fit 40 people inside.

- Peanuts grow underground, making them legumes rather than nuts.

- Members of the peach family include almonds.

- Strawberries are not a berry, but bananas are.

- Up to one billion pollen grains can be produced by a single ragweed plant.

- Because of the shape of the plant's root, the word "orchid" derives from a Greek word that means "testicle."

- In reality, coffee beans are berry pits.

- Compared to people, tomatoes have more genes.

- The fruit known as a pineapple is actually a collection of berries that have grown together.

- Plants can recognize their siblings and treat them preferentially so that competition for coveted resources like root space is reduced.

- There is only one Kaikmako manawa twhi tree left in the world, and it is growing wild in New Zealand.

- Red sap that resembles blood is produced by the Dragon's blood tree.

- The cashew apple is the fruit from which cashews are derived.

- Eucalyptus trees are explosive during bushfires and highly flammable.

- Some plants, such as the "snake plant," carry out photosynthesis at night.

- After being consumed, certain "Zombie plants" can control an animal's behavior.

- Tulip bulbs were more expensive than gold in the Netherlands in the 1600s.

- 'Ophiocordyceps unilateralis' is a fungus that infects ants and takes over their bodies.

- The original source of the painkiller aspirin was the bark of willow trees.

- Some plants, like mustard, produce chemicals as a defense mechanism against herbivores.

- Birds are poisoned by avocados.

- The parasitic mistletoe can kill the host tree by depriving it of nutrients and water.

- Approximately 75,000 crocus flowers are required to produce one pound of the common spice saffron, which is derived from the stigma of the flower.

- The oceans are home to more than 85% of all plant life on Earth.

- Known as Methuselah, the oldest living tree is over 4,800 years old and can be found in the White Mountains of California.

- The smallest flowering plant, known as a 'wolffia," resembles tiny grains of rice and can grow on the surface of water.

- A tree's bark is where most of its nutrients are kept.

- Male pinecones expel pollen, while female pinecones

produce seeds. Pinecones have gender.

- Up to 20 feet tall, the tequila agave plant's flower stalk can resemble a tree.

- Like a warm-blooded animal, the lotus flower can control its body temperature.

- Tonic water's bitter flavor comes from the quinine, which was first used to treat malaria and is derived from the cinchona tree's bark.

- The leaves of the 'sensitive plant' (Mimosa pudica) fold inward in response to touch.

- Rafflesia arnoldii, the largest flower in the world, has a three-foot diameter.

- A desert plant known as the "living stone" is so named because it closely resembles the rocks it grows among

- Except for one type, which is native to Africa, cacti are only found in the Americas.

Crazy Animal Facts

- Human faces can be recognized by honeybees.

- Starfish do not have brains.

- A shrimp's head is where its heart is.

- Because they are cube-shaped, wombat faeces cannot roll away.

- A snail's sleep can last up to three years.

- Koala fingerprints are so similar to human fingerprints that they have baffled crime scene investigators.

- Cows have best friends.

- The male seahorse gives birth to and carries the young.

- Butterflies use their feet to taste.

- An albatross can nap while flying.

- A "flamboyance" is the name for a group of flamingos.

- Hair that has been compressed makes up a rhinoceros' horn.

- An octopus has a parrot-like beak.

- Because frogs are unable to vomit, when they consume poison, their entire stomach is ejected.

- Dolphins give each other names.

- Elephant teeth can weigh as much as 9 pounds each.

- Penguins can drink seawater because they have a gland that removes salt from their bloodstream.

- Fifty people could stand on the blue whale's enormous tongue.

- Crows can distinguish between distinct human faces, as well as harboring grudges.

- A crocodile is unable to extend its tongue.

- Rainstorms can be heard by elephants from up to 150 miles away.

- The giraffe's neck has the same number of vertebrae as a human does.

- Armadillos can swim.

- One meal, for a sloth, takes about a month to digest.

- Cheetahs chirp like birds instead of roaring.

- As a form of defense, some lizards can squirt blood from their eyes.

- The axolotl can regrow parts of its brain, spine, heart, and even limbs.

- The key of F is the hum of houseflies.

- The eye of an ostrich is larger than the brain.

- The amount of darkness in a lion's mane can be used to estimate its age.

- A baby duck is known as a duckling, a female duck is known as a hen, and a male duck is known as a drake.

- The bumblebee bat, which weighs just 2 grammes and is 1 to 1.3 inches long, is the tiniest mammal in the world.

- The only mammals that have been found to lay eggs are the platypus and echidna.

- A chameleon's tongue is twice as long as its body.

- Polar bears have black skin and translucent, not white, fur.

- The bat is the only mammal capable of sustained flight.

- Over 50 different types of bacteria can be found in a Komodo dragon's saliva, which is lethal to its prey.

- Naked mole-rats are immune to cancer.

- To prevent drifting apart while they sleep, sea otters hold hands.

- The mantis shrimp has bullet-like punching speed.

- Fleas can accelerate 50 times more quickly than a space

shuttle.

- The male mosquito only consumes nectar and does not bite.

- Dogs are not as smart as pigs.

- A cricket's front legs are home to its ears.

- A hummingbird weighs less than a penny.

- Puffins scratch their bodies with twigs.

- The color of a reindeer's eyes changes with the seasons.

- A "pandemonium" of parrots is a collection of them.

- Horses and rats cannot throw up.

- Dragonflies only live for about 24 hours.

- The blobfish does not resemble a blob in its natural environment. The gelatinous appearance is caused by the pressure change.

- Vultures can digest anthrax due to their extremely corrosive stomach acids.

Wonderous Weather

- The driest, windiest, and coldest continent on Earth is Antarctica.

- A single lightning bolt can heat the air around it to 30,000°C and travels at a speed of about 270,000 mph.

- 56.7°C (134°F) was the highest temperature ever recorded in 1913 at Furnace Creek Ranch in Death Valley, California.

- 89.2°C (128.6°F) was the lowest natural temperature ever directly measured at Earth's surface in Antarctica in 1983.

- When luminous plasma forms on pointed objects during thunderstorms, it is known as St. Elmo's fire.

- Mawsynram, in India, is the wettest place on Earth, with an average annual rainfall of 467.4 inches.

- A cumulus cloud weighs about 1.1 million pounds.

- Until they pick up debris or a cloud forms inside the funnel, tornadoes may not be visible.

- Despite being extremely hot during the day, the Sahara Desert can drop to 30°F at night.

- For two months in 1684, the River Thames in England was completely frozen over.

- There are 35 different shapes of snowflakes.

- The Earth's record-breaking wind speed was 253 mph, which occurred in an Oklahoma tornado in 1999.

- There are parts of Chile's Atacama Desert where no rain has ever been observed.

- A cloud that touches the ground creates fog.

- Up to three million volts can be measured in a lightning strike.

- Typhoons, cyclones, and hurricanes are all different names for the same weather phenomenon, they just occur in different locations.

- In 2001, Kansas experienced a rain of tiny frogs, a rare meteorological phenomenon.

- A heat burst is a rare instance where evening temperatures increase rather than decrease.

- A brief period of glowing, floating lightning known as "ball lightning" can last several seconds.

- Temperatures can rise by up to 40°F in just a few minutes thanks to chinook winds.

- The McMurdo Dry Valleys in Antarctica, where there has not been a drop of rain for nearly 2 million years, are the driest place on Earth.

- The high pressure and carbon-rich atmosphere of Jupiter and Saturn may cause diamonds to rain from the sky.

- One of the coldest places to live is the Russian town of Oymyakon.

- Tornadoes that form over water are known as waterspouts.

- The sun or moon's halo is a result of high, thin cirrus clouds that reflect light.

- Mamatus clouds have the appearance of pouches dangling from their undersides.

- An enormous dust storm is a haboob.

- Ice storms are instances in which everything is covered in an ice layer by freezing rain.

- Every minute, there are about 2,000 thunderstorms on Earth.

- There is no wind and an unnerving calm inside the eye of a hurricane.

- The largest hailstone ever recorded fell in South Dakota in 2010 and weighted nearly 2 pounds.

- The phrase "dog days of summer" comes from the prehistoric idea that Sirius, the Dog Star, was to blame for the sweltering conditions.

- Green flashes that last only a few seconds occasionally appear just after dusk or just before dawn.

- Rainbows that appear at night are known as moonbows.

- A tornado's typical life span is just ten minutes.

- Microbursts and sudden downdrafts can cause more damage than tornadoes.

- The English town of Sutton experienced a rain of fish in 1954.

- A hiatus is defined as a decade without any observed global warming.

- The Krakatoa volcano eruption in 1883 caused a long-lasting change in the hue of sunsets all over the world.

- Due to severe air pollution, the Great Smog of 1952 in London resulted in thousands of fatalities.

- In 1985, the ozone layer's hole was discovered.

- A thick dew called white frost develops when the air temperature falls below freezing.

- Graupel is a type of soft hail or snow powder.

- The Coriolis effect causes moving air and water to turn and twist in certain predictable patterns.

- Coalescence occurs when two raindrops combine as they fall.

- Volcanic eruptions caused the "Year Without a Summer" of 1816.

- In Iran, a blizzard dumped 26 feet of snow in 1972.

- Collisions between charged solar particles and gaseous particles in the Earth's atmosphere give rise to the Aurora Borealis and Aurora Australis.

- An intense area of sunlight that is occasionally visible 22° to the left or right of the sun is known as a sun dog.

- A mackerel sky is filled with rows of cirrocumulus or altocumulus clouds displaying an undulating, rippling pattern similar in appearance to fish scales.

- The Sirocco wind spreads dusty, dry conditions across places like North Africa and Southern Europe.

- Complex weather patterns like El Nio and La Nia are brought on by changes in ocean temperatures.

Ecosystems

- 20% of the oxygen in the world is produced by the Amazon Rainforest.

- Coral reefs occupy less than 0.1% of the world's ocean surface, yet they provide a habitat for 25% of all marine species.

- The largest terrestrial biome on earth, the Taiga, also known as the Boreal Forest, spans Canada, Russia, and Scandinavia.

- After Antarctica and the Arctic, the Sahara Desert is the third-largest desert with a total area of over 9 million square kilometers.

- At the bottom of the ocean, there are lakes and rivers that have shorelines and waves.

- 25% of the Earth's surface is made up of grasslands, which are home to many large herbivores like elephants and bison.

- Wetlands store three times as much carbon as a tropical forest, making them the most effective carbon sinks on Earth.

- Only 5% of the oceans on Earth have been thoroughly studied.

- More than half of the species in the world live in rainforests.

- Since the Dead Sea is ten times saltier than the ocean, most life cannot exist there.

- Mountains have alpine ecosystems that begin where the growth of trees ceases.

- The deep sea is home to the planet's largest ecosystem, which is mostly unexplored.

- Mangroves, tropical trees that can survive in saltwater, are the most effective forests for storing carbon dioxide.

- Parts of California have chaparral ecosystems, which are characterized by shrubby plants adapted to wet winters and dry summers.

- The amount of carbon dioxide in Arctic permafrost is twice that of the atmosphere.

- The most productive ecosystems are found in estuaries, which are where rivers and oceans meet.

- Glaciers hold about 70% of the freshwater on Earth.

- An ecosystem without trees, the tundra can be found in cold climates with short growing seasons.

- To save water, trees in temperate deciduous forests lose their leaves in the autumn.

- After the Amazon and the Congo, Indonesia has the third-largest rainforest in the world.

- The largest tropical wilderness in the United States is the Everglades in Florida.

- Diverse marine species can be found in kelp forests, which are underwater regions where kelp is present in large quantities.

- Ecosystems in caves depend on nutrients brought in from outside and do not receive any sunlight.

- Many endangered species, including giant pandas, can be found in bamboo forests.

- Ancient bristlecone pine forests are home to some of the oldest organisms on earth.

- Compared to other rivers on the planet, the Amazon River discharges five times as much water.

- Many of the most well-known wild animals in the world, such as lions, elephants, and giraffes, can be found in savannas, which are grasslands with sporadic trees.

- Although the Amazon is frequently referred to as the "lungs of the Earth," the plankton in the world's oceans also contributes an equal or greater amount of oxygen.

- The largest living organism on Earth is a honey fungus that covers over 2,400 acres in Oregon.

- The largest tropical wetland in the world is in South America's Pantanal.

- In Central and South America, you can find more than half of the world's tropical rainforests.

Dexter Informa's Interesting Facts About Nature

- A handful of forest soil contains more microorganisms than there are people on the planet.

- Mountainous areas with cloud forests experience nearly constant 100% humidity.

- Temperate rainforests, found in cooler climates, have mosses and lichens growing on tree trunks.

- The Chaparral biome has plants that recover quickly from burns and are adapted to periodic fires.

- In some deep-sea ecosystems, bacteria use sulphur as energy instead of sunlight.

- There are over 100,000 known species of plants and animals that live in freshwater ecosystems.

- Ecosystems around hydrothermal vents in the depths of the ocean lack sunlight and rely on chemosynthesis.

- Around 80% of plants on Earth produce flowers.

- Cacti, a type of desert plant, can store water and are able to withstand high temperatures.

- Deep roots in grasslands help to stop soil erosion.

- In a phenomenon called "leaf flushing," a forest changes its color due to new leaf growth.

- The densely wooded Black Forest in Germany is the setting of numerous folklore and legends.

- Although 90% of Madagascar's forests have been destroyed,

its ecosystems still contain 5% of the world's total biodiversity.

- For young fish, seagrass meadows are essential nurseries.

- 10% of the freshwater on the planet is found in the Arctic.

- The thick trunks of baobab trees, which grow in the African savannah, are used to store water.

- Over a million wildebeest and zebras migrate through the Serengeti in Africa every year, which is the largest migration event on Earth.

- Ten percent of the freshwater on Earth is stored in peat bogs.

- The Netherlands has a quarter of its land below sea level, and a large portion of its land has been reclaimed from the sea.

- The Sundarbans, which straddles Bangladesh and India, is the largest mangrove forest in the world.

- The term "plastisphere" describes ecosystems that have developed to coexist peacefully with oceanic plastic waste.

- Some of the tallest sand dunes in the world can be found in the Namib Desert.

- Due to a particular kind of algae, some lakes in Australia have a pink coloration by nature.

- Freshwater lakes, like Lake Kaindy in Kazakhstan, have underwater forests.

- A region in the Pacific Ocean basin known as the "Ring of

Fire" experiences frequent earthquakes and volcanic eruptions.

- The distinctive ecosystems of the Galápagos Islands were crucial to Charles Darwin's theory of evolution.

- In comparison to plants, fungi are more closely related to animals.

- 20% of the freshwater on earth is found in Lake Baikal, the deepest freshwater lake in the world, which is in Russia.

- Real animals that inhabit glaciers are known as ice worms.

- The Gobi Desert is growing by over 1,300 square miles per year, a phenomenon known as desertification.

Under the Microscope

- 20% of the oxygen on Earth is produced by diatoms, tiny algae with walls resembling glass.

- Your mouth contains more bacteria than there are people on the planet.

- Water bears, also referred to as Tardigrades, are tiny creatures that can endure space's vacuum.

- Bacteria are typically only 1 micron in size. If there were 1000 of them lined up, they would measure just 1 millimeter in length.

- A grain of sand is 500 times larger than the flu virus.

- Despite being single-celled, slime molds can navigate mazes by choosing the quickest path to food.

- The Pithovirus sibericum, the largest known virus, was found in Siberian permafrost and is more than 30,000 years old.

- The first antibiotic ever discovered, penicillin, was made from the mold Penicillium.

- E. coli bacteria can divide and reproduce every 20 minutes.

- Billions of microorganisms can be found in a single gram of soil.

- Some bacteria have pili, which resemble hairs and are used to attach to surfaces.

- A bacterium known as Deinococcus radiodurans is capable of enduring extreme radiation, cold, dehydration, and the vacuum of space.

- Many scientists disagree that viruses are alive because they cannot reproduce on their own.

- The human body is host to trillions of microbes, collectively known as the microbiome.

- Given that they have existed for more than 2.5 billion years, cyanobacteria are some of the planet's oldest living things.

- The fungi kingdom is more closely related to animals than they are to plants.

- Some fungi interact mutualistically with plants, exchanging nutrients.

- Yeast, which is a type of fungus, is used to ferment beer and make bread rise.

- Extreme environments, such as icy polar regions, acidic lakes, and deep-sea vents, are home to bacteria.

- Some bacteria can photosynthesize like plants.

- It is possible for bioluminescent bacteria to produce light.

- The giant squid has the largest known eye in the animal kingdom, but the bacteria that live on its surface are just a fraction of a millimeter in size.

- The number of bacteria and viruses in a single drop of seawater is in the millions.

- Bacteria, which are very small, were the first life forms on Earth.

- Solibacillus kalamii is a species of bacterium that was found on the International Space Station.

- Since the single-celled organisms known as Archaea can produce methane, they are frequently referred to as methanogens.

- Bioluminescence is a phenomenon that occurs when certain types of plankton produce light.

- A type of bacteria called Helicobacter pylori has been linked to ulcers because it can survive in the acidic environment of the stomach.

- Amoebas move using pseudopods, which are temporary protrusions of their cell membrane.

- Radiolarians, microscopic organisms with intricate silica skeletons, have existed for over 500 million years.

- Ants can become infected with fungi that take over their

nervous systems and force them to climb plants before the fungus explodes from their heads.

- The lytic cycle is the process by which a virus enters and commandeers the functional components of a host cell.

- Foraminifera, tiny marine organisms, build shells called tests which have been preserved in sediments, providing a record of past climates.

- Enzymes derived from bacteria are commonly found in laundry detergents and are used to dissolve biological stains.

- There are 400–500 different bacterial species found in the human gut.

- Microscopic creatures known as bdelloid rotifers have not reproduced sexually for millions of years.

- Infected insects can change their sex thanks to a type of bacteria called Wolbachia.

- Snowflakes develop around microscopic dust particles in the air.

- The human brain can become infected by a species of fungus known as Cryptococcus neoformans.

- Phages are viruses that infect only bacteria.

- One of the tiniest known bacteria, Mycoplasma genitalium only has 525 genes.

- Some bacteria, such as those in the genus Clostridium, can endure harsh environments for an extended period thanks to the endospores they produce.

- The oldest fossils that have been discovered are bacteria-like organisms, dating back more than 3.5 billion years.

- Cilia are specialized structures used by single-celled organisms called paramecia to move and feed.

- Legumes' roots contain bacteria that aid in the conversion of atmospheric nitrogen into a form that plants can utilize.

- An instance of micro-evolution is the development of bacteria that are resistant to the effects of antibiotics.

- The first virus to be completely vanquished by a vaccine was the smallpox virus.

- Some bacteria are electrically conductors and could be utilized in biotechnologies in the future.

- Antonie van Leeuwenhoek was the first to use a microscope to view bacteria in 1675.

- The yeast species that is most frequently used in baking and brewing is Saccharomyces cerevisiae.

- Due to its heat resistance, the bacterium Thermus aquaticus, which is discovered in Yellowstone's hot springs, is utilized in the PCR DNA replication process.

- Microorganisms referred to as "extremophiles" thrive in conditions with high salinity, acidity, or temperature.

- Diatoms' fossilized remains are used to create diatomaceous earth, which is used in numerous products.

- Some bacteria can communicate by releasing signaling molecules during a process known as quorum sensing.

- By dissolving organic matter, fungi play a significant part in ecosystems.

- The "Wood Wide Web" is a term that has been used to describe the fungus network that links plant roots in forests.

- Around 8 million tons of plastic end up in the ocean each year, and microscopic plastic particles are ingested by marine life.

- 2018 saw the discovery of the marine parasite Hemimastix kukwesjijk, which does not belong to any known kingdom of life.

- Giardia is a microscopic parasite that can survive for months and causes digestive disorders.

- Spores, which are used by fungi to reproduce, can travel great distances in the air.

- The number of ribosomes in a single bacterial cell can reach 10 million.

- Despite its name, the golden algae can have a green, brown, red, or even blue appearance depending on the environment.

- The word "plankton" comes from the Greek word "planktos," which is a synonym for "wanderer" or "drifter."

Geography

- The only continent situated in all four hemispheres is Africa.

- The Dead Sea is about eight times as salty as the ocean.

- Istanbul, Turkey, lies on both the European and Asian Continents.

- Only about 6,000 of Indonesia's 17,500 islands are inhabited.

- With a land area of only 44 hectares, Vatican City is the smallest nation in the world.

- There are 11 time zones in Russia.

- Taumatawhakatangi-hangakoauauotamatea-turipukakapikima unga-horonukupokaiwhen-uakitanatahu, which is in New Zealand, has the longest place name.

- The Sahara Desert greater in area than the entire U.S. continent.

- The Amazon River discharges 5 times the volume of water as any other river on the planet.

- The Northern Hemisphere is home to 90% of the world's inhabitants.

- Tectonic forces cause Mount Everest to grow by about 4 millimeters every year.

- In Norway, there is a town called "Hell," and each winter it freezes over.

- Britain and Zanzibar engaged in the shortest war in history in 1896. After 38 minutes, Zanzibar surrendered.

- The farthest point from any land is in the Pacific Ocean at a place called Point Nemo. The astronauts on the International Space Station are frequently the closest humans to its inhabitants.

- Monaco is smaller than Central Park in New York City.

- As the longest railway in the world, the Trans-Siberian Railway stretches almost the entire length of Russia.

- The San Marino Republic, established in A.D. 301, is the oldest republic still in existence.

- From the Moon, you cannot see the Great Wall of China with the naked eye. It is a myth.

- Over 800 languages are thought to be spoken in Papua New Guinea.

- The largest tropical lake in the world is Lake Victoria in Africa.

- The United States is home to one-third of all airports in the world.

- The oldest and deepest freshwater lake, which was mentioned earlier in this book, is in Russia and is named Lake Baikal.

- Microsoft's corporate headquarters in Washington state houses the quietest room in the world.

- The closest spot on Earth to the moon is Mount Chimborazo in Ecuador.

- More lakes exist in Canada than there are in the entire rest of the world.

- The longest unbroken land route is the Pan-American Highway, running from Alaska to Argentina but interrupted by a 100-mile gap in Panama and Colombia.

- Only Lesotho, Vatican City, and San Marino are entirely surrounded by another nation.

- The "White Shark Café" is a location in the Pacific Ocean where sharks eerily congregate every year.

- The world's largest island is Greenland.

- In terms of elevation, Amsterdam is the lowest national capital in the entire world.

- The Mediterranean Sea and the Red Sea are linked by Egypt's Suez Canal.

- The Siachen Glacier, which is halfway between Pakistan and India, is the highest battleground in the world.

- With a length of more than 7,000 kilometers, the Andes are the longest mountain range in the world.

- The Grand Canyon can hold around 900 trillion footballs.

- The Atacama Desert is the driest place on Earth; in some areas, there has not been any significant precipitation for nearly 400 years.

- The Amazon River is fed by more than 200 rivers.

- One of the coldest towns on the planet is Oymyakon in Russia.

- In a town in Norway, it is against the law to pass away because the frozen ground prevents burials.

- No map recognizes the Bermuda Triangle as an official location.

- The Netherlands has 40% of its land below sea level.

- The Sargasso Sea is the only ocean without a land border.

- Only the continents of Asia and Africa have the Prime Meridian and the Equator running through them.

- Saudi Arabia does not have any rivers.

- Llanfairpwllgwyngyll-gogery-chwyrn-drobwll-llan-tysilio-gogo-g och is the name of a town in Wales.

- The highest continuous waterfall in the world is Angel Falls in Venezuela.

- In the Caribbean, there are more than 7,000 distinct islands.

- The fourth-largest island in the world and the largest in the Indian Ocean is Madagascar.

- With all its fjords and inlets, Norway's coastline covers more than 25,000 kilometers.

- The "Zealandia" continent, which includes New Zealand, is 93% underwater.

- While the Pacific Ocean is getting smaller every year, the Atlantic Ocean is expanding.

- The highest temperature ever measured on Earth's surface was 56.7°C (134°F) in Death Valley, USA, at Furnace Creek Ranch.

- With 14 bordering nations, China is the nation with the most neighbors.

- The only continent without an active volcano is Australia.

- Yes, Australia is a continent.

- The length of the equator, which separates the Earth's hemispheres into the northern and southern, is about 40,075 kilometers.

- In terms of surface area, the Pacific Ocean dwarfs the planet's entire landmass.

- By 2050, 25% of the world's population will reside in Africa.

- One of the hottest and most hostile places on Earth is Ethiopia's Danakil Depression.

- The Tree of Ténéré, once found in the Sahara Desert, was the most remote tree on earth. In 1973, a truck struck it and knocked it to the ground.

- The Yarlung Tsangpo Grand Canyon, the largest canyon in the world, is deeper and longer than the Grand Canyon and is situated in the Himalayas.

- Turkmenistan's "Door to Hell" natural gas field has been burning since 1971.

Nature Through Our Own Eyes

- Early agricultural practices were used by the ancient Egyptians as early as 6000 BC.

- The Amazon Rainforest has been shaped in part by human activity for over 11,000 years.

- The Japanese practice of "forest bathing," or shinrin-yoku, involves immersing oneself in nature to enhance health.

- Some cultures have a tradition of honey hunting, which involves gathering honey from wild beehives. This tradition dates back thousands of years.

- Early examples of vertical gardening can be found in the Hanging Gardens of Babylon, one of the Seven Wonders of the Ancient World.

- Poor agricultural practices in the 1930s exacerbated the Dust Bowl.

- The use of natural elements in architectural design, or "biophilic design," can enhance mental health.

- Since the 1950s, more than 8.3 billion tons of plastic have been produced by humans, much of it ending up in the environment.

- Cities like Detroit and Tokyo are setting the standard for cutting-edge agricultural practices, with urban farming on the rise.

- Early Polynesians traveled great distances in canoes by using the stars, wind, and ocean currents.

- To prevent crop extinction, samples of seeds from all over the world are kept in a "seed vault" in Svalbard, Norway.

- Crop rotation was a technique used by the ancient Greeks to increase soil fertility.

- For thousands of years, indigenous communities have used controlled burns to manage their land.

- The term "nature deficit disorder" refers to problems with human health brought on by disconnection from the natural world.

- Yellowstone, which is in the United States, became the first national park ever created in 1872.

- Animals flourished in the evacuated area after the Chernobyl nuclear disaster in 1986, which unintentionally created a wildlife sanctuary.

- According to NASA's Clean Air Study, plants like the Peace Lily can purify indoor air.

- The Native Americans' planting method of 'three sisters' entails growing corn, beans, and squash next to each other for mutual benefit.

- From the grey wolf, humans have domesticated more than 340 different dog breeds.

- Guano, or bird droppings, was a vital agricultural product and a source of fertilizer in the 19th century.

- In many cultures, the custom of planting according to the phases of the moon is still prevalent.

- Farming was possible on mountain slopes thanks to the historic practice of constructing terraced fields, like those in Machu Picchu.

- On a smaller scale, traditional Chinese gardens are made to resemble natural landscapes.

- According to some studies, "earthing," or going barefoot on natural surfaces, can lower stress.

- Fern collecting in Victorian England became such a craze that it was given the name "pteridomania."

- Animal trails have influenced the design of some hiking paths and city layouts.

- Bird flight served as an inspiration for Leonardo da Vinci's early designs for flying machines.

- In urban areas around the world, rooftop gardens are growing in popularity because they offer insulation as well as fresh produce.

- The Dutch have been pioneers in using windmills and dikes to reclaim land from the sea.

- Childhood fantasies of treehouses have their origins in indigenous cultures, where they were used to keep out wild animals.

- More than 30 underwater cities have been built in Japan to preserve marine life and slow the sea level rise.

- The ancient Incas created Moray, a location with elliptical terraces that may have served as an agricultural research facility.

- By reducing waste and planting trees, music festivals like Tomorrowland are integrating sustainability.

- Global awareness and appreciation of nature have been influenced by Sir David Attenborough's documentaries.

- Outdoor activities are incorporated into therapeutic procedures through "ecotherapy".

- The Great Green Wall project aims to stop desertification by creating a wall of trees across Africa.

- Due to the release of a substance called "phytoncides" by plants, humans can identify specific smells in a forest.

- In 2012, India planted 50 million trees in a single day,

breaking the previous record.

- Hawaiian natives invented surfing, which is now a popular sport worldwide.

- In order to reduce pollution, vertical forests—skyscrapers covered in trees—are being constructed in cities like Milan.

- The concept of national parks has its roots in indigenous land stewardship practices.

- Gross National Happiness, which places value on environmental preservation, is measured in Bhutan.

- Norway pays Liberia to stop deforestation.

- The Great Barrier Reef is the largest living structure created by an organism other than a human.

- A complex system was created by the ancient Nabateans in what is now Jordan to collect and store desert rainwater.

- Some farmers use classical music to promote the growth of their crops and livestock.

- To create sustainable farming systems, "agroforestry" combines trees and shrubs with crops and livestock.

- Planting without permission on vacant urban land is known as "guerrilla gardening," and it is a type of environmental activism.

- Replicating nature in miniature is a key component of the ancient art of bonsai.

- Rain dances and ceremonies were performed in many cultures to call for rain.

- Indigenous Australians used "songlines," or singing tracks, to travel across vast lands.

- African Maasai traditionally build their homes out of mud, sticks, grass, cow dung, and cow urine.

- A design method known as "permaculture" uses natural patterns to build livable environments and efficient food production systems.

- On the cave walls, prehistoric humans painted pictures of animals, the outdoors, and hunts.

- Collaboration is used in the Dutch "polder model" to manage and keep water off their submerged lands.

- Because of their spiritual significance, trees are revered and protected in some cultures.

- Some Native American cultures use vision quests as a form of rite of passage that entails solitary immersion in the natural world.

- Along with trade, the well-known Silk Road promoted the exchange of agricultural knowledge and plant species.

- To combat urban heat, cities like Singapore are incorporating "green buildings" that are covered in plants.

- People rely on coral reefs for resources and coastal

protection even though they only make up a small portion of the ocean floor—less than 1%.

- The Māori people of New Zealand see themselves as "kaitiaki," or guardians, of the environment.

- The British obsession with landscape gardening in the 18th century wanted to resemble wild nature.

- Initiatives known as "rewilding" aim to return areas to their untamed, undeveloped state.

- In many cultures, it is customary to plant a tree when a child is born to represent life and growth.

- Dams, like the Hoover Dam or Three Gorges in China, demonstrate human engineering transforming natural waterways.

Unexplained Nature

- There have been several mysterious ship and aircraft disappearances that have been connected to the Bermuda Triangle, which is in the western North Atlantic Ocean.

- The "sailing stones" of Death Valley National Park move independently and leave footprints, while researchers believe that tiny sheets of ice might be involved.

- A small percentage of the inhabitants of Taos, New Mexico, have reported hearing the Taos Hum, a low-frequency sound that is currently unexplained.

- The Marfa Lights of Texas are mysterious glowing orbs that appear in the desert, with theories ranging from atmospheric reflections to ghost lights.

- No one knows the real reason the chicken crossed the road, despite its storied past.

- Some birds like European robins might use quantum entanglement in their eyes for migration, but the exact process remains a mystery.

- Numerous explanations exist for the round, desert-covered areas known as fairy circles, ranging from termite activity to plant water competition.

- Unknown symbols and illustrations of unidentified plants can be found in the Voynich manuscript, a mediaeval book which has still not been deciphered.

- Red rain has been reported in various locations across the world, and its causes have been attributed to everything from desert dust to extraterrestrial origins.

- The Naga fireballs, glowing balls that rise from the Mekong River in Thailand, are an unexplained phenomenon thought by some to be dragon breath.

- Bigfoot, sometimes known as Sasquatch, is a supposedly ape-like creature that has been reported in North America but is yet to be proven by reliable evidence.

- Theories about crop circles, complex designs that suddenly arise in farmers' fields, range from hoaxes to extraterrestrial art.

- Believed to live in Loch Ness in the Scottish Highlands, the Loch Ness Monster has been seen several times since the 1930s but is still elusive.

- Trees were presumably destroyed by a meteor explosion during the "Tunguska event" in Siberia in 1908, but no impact crater was ever discovered.

- In 1966, the residents of Taured arrived at Tokyo airport with a passport from a country that does not exist.

- The "Wow! signal," a radio transmission from space that was discovered in 1977, lasted 72 seconds and is still unaccounted for.

- Animal rain, wherein little animals like fish or frogs fall from the sky, has been observed all over the world. It may be caused by updrafts; however, this is frequently a mystery to specialists.

- There are mysterious "star jelly" deposits that occasionally occur overnight and are frequently associated with meteor showers but have no clear explanation.

- Magnetic fields and UFO activity are two ideas for the "zone of silence" in Mexico, where radio transmissions do not work.

- There is controversy over whether the "Yonaguni Monument," an underwater rock formation near Japan, is a natural or an old man-made construction.

- Scientists are still unsure of why the "Black Dahlia" plants' blossoms have an unsettling metallic shimmer.

- The authenticity of the Patterson-Gimlin footage, a 1967 film clip that purports to show Bigfoot in California, is still up for question.

- Although meteorite impacts are thought to have created some "desert glass" found in places like the Sahara, the origin of some pieces is still unexplained.

- With unknown effects from space flight, "Moon trees," or trees cultivated from seeds brought to the moon during the Apollo 14 mission, have been planted all over the planet.

- The "long-delayed echoes," or radio transmissions that arrive on Earth after a delay, are still an enigma.

- It is unclear how the bacteria manage to thrive in the flow of iron-rich, salty water known as the "blood falls" in Antarctica.

- Possibly produced by an icequake or an unidentified massive marine organism, the "Bloop" was an ultra-low-frequency sound that was heard in the Pacific Ocean in 1997.

- There are many different explanations for the mysterious shimmering orbs known as "Min Min lights" in Australia, from bioluminescence to mirages.

- There are clones of some trees, such the "Old Tjikko" in Sweden, whose root systems have survived for more than 9,500 years.

- Research is still being done to determine how "blue holes," or deep blue underwater sinkholes, originate.

- Scientists are baffled by "Klerksdorp spheres," tiny spherical objects discovered in granite that is 3 billion years old, yet others think they are naturally occurring concretions.

- There have long been rumors about "phantom islands," or

land masses that have vanished from maps but were formerly thought to exist.

- The "Devil's Kettle," a waterfall in Minnesota that divides in two and has one side that sinks beneath the ground, obscures its final location.

- Some ancient rock art depicts figures or patterns that do not correspond to known cultures or creatures.

- The reason of the twisted trunks and rings on the pine trees in Russia's enigmatic "Dancing Forest" is unknown.

- There are optical illusions and gravitational anomalies in the Oregon Vortex, a popular tourist destination.

- "Underwater crop circles" created by male pufferfish to attract females were only discovered in 1995.

- Unidentified sounds emanating from the ground in Connecticut are known as "Moodus noises," and they have been connected to local myths and seismic activity.

- There is no universal agreement on the causes of the "Singing Sand" phenomena, which causes sand dunes to make musical noises.

- It is still unclear why the Southeast Asian mammal known as the binturong smells like buttered popcorn.

- Magnetic hills or roads that seem to defy gravity can be found in numerous places, where vehicles seem to roll uphill.

- The enigma surrounding the "Green Children of Woolpit," a legend from the Middle Ages about youngsters with green skin who appeared in England, is still unsolved to this day.

- Many doubts remain regarding some creatures' migratory tendencies, such as the Arctic tern's 12,000-mile trek.

- Some ancient geoglyphs and petroglyphs feature figures that can only be seen from a great height, raising concerns about the intentions of their makers.

- The origins of the mysterious glowing orbs known as "Spooklights" in Missouri are unknown.

- Three coded communications from the 1820s known as the "Beale cyphers," which are claimed to lead to treasure, are still unsolved.

- In some regions of Asia, the origins of strange stone jars that are thought to be more than 2,000 years old are unclear.

- The "Eternal Flame Falls" in New York has a natural gas vent under a waterfall that keeps a flame burning.

- People all throughout the world are experiencing the "Hum," which is a persistent low-frequency noise with no obvious source.

- It is still unclear what causes the "Ball lightning" occurrence, which involves glowing orbs in thunderstorms.

- Some ancient structures, like Sacsayhuamán in Peru, have

massive stones fitted so precisely that they baffle modern engineers.

- The "Antikythera mechanism," an ancient Greek analog computer, hints at technological sophistication beyond its era.

- Since the 1930s, the mystery surrounding the "Hessdalen lights" in Norway—unexplained lights that emerge in a particular valley—has persisted.

- Off the Yucatan coast, the "disappearing island" of Bermeja was previously mapped but has since disappeared.

- The origins of the circular patterns which are visible from the air, known as "Forest rings" in Ontario are unknown, however fungal activity is thought to be a possibility.

- The "Mary Celeste" was discovered drifting in 1872, unmanned but in good sailing condition.

- The "Origin of the Moon" is the subject of numerous theories, ranging from massive collisions to geysers, with no collective agreement of how it happened.

- Numerous nearly perfect spherical stones, known as "Stone Balls of Costa Rica," have mysterious origins.

- Worldwide reports of "Skyquakes," tremendous booms from the sky that have no clear cause, have been made.

- The "Shugborough inscription," a coded sequence of letters on a monument in England, remains undeciphered.

- A creature seen before the Chernobyl catastrophe, the "Blackbird of Chernobyl," is now included in the list of unsolved cryptids.

- It is possible that the "sea monsters" depicted on old maps, which sometimes look like huge serpents, are based on myths, or incorrectly identified species.

- With hypotheses ranging from deep-sea vents to extraterrestrial seeds, the "Origin of Life" is still one of the greatest mysteries.

- There are several theoretical explanations for the "Overtoun Bridge" in Scotland, where countless dogs have jumped to their deaths.

Evolution

- Single-celled organisms are thought to have started life on Earth around 3.5 billion years ago.

- Western Australia is home to the oldest fossils, called stromatolites, which were created by bacteria and algae.

- About 541 million years ago, during the Cambrian Explosion, there was an abrupt increase in the variety of life forms over a comparatively short period of geological time.

- Fungi predominated on Earth before trees, some of which grew to be as tall as trees and created prehistoric "mushroom forests."

- Trilobites, which are extinct now, inhabited the oceans for more than 270 million years and left behind a wealth of fossils.

- The emergence of aerobic life and the production of oxygen as a byproduct of photosynthesis fundamentally altered the Earth's atmosphere.

- Dinosaurs roamed the Earth for about 165 million years, a period much longer than humans have been around.

- Birds are the modern-day descendants of theropod dinosaurs, like the T. rex.

- Nearly 90% of all species were exterminated during the Permian period's mass extinction, which happened about 252 million years ago.

- Around 5-7 million years ago, our human lineage diverged from chimpanzees, the closest living relatives of ours.

- Early primates' development of an opposable thumb changed the game by making it easier to use tools.

- Around 50 million years ago, whales were four-legged land animals; during their evolutionary transition to the oceans, vestiges of their leg bones were left behind.

- Because the first mammals lived primarily at night, we have less developed color vision than many other animals.

- The asteroid impact that wiped out the dinosaurs also made way for mammals to take control, including humans.

- Caffeine is a natural defense mechanism that some plants have developed to paralyze and kill insect predators.

- Lizards are capable of parthenogenetic reproduction, or "virgin births," where females reproduce devoid of male partners.

- Fruit developed as a result of a mutualistic relationship between plants and animals, who dispersed seeds in exchange for food from the plants.

- Some species of snakes still have remnants of their once four-legged ancestors' leg bones.

- The narwhal's recognizable "horns" are actually long, elongated teeth that can grow up to 10 feet long.

- The single-toed hooves of the modern horse evolved from multi-toed ancestors.

- Argentinosaurus, the largest land animal ever to roam the earth, lived 94 million years ago and could weigh up to 100 tons.

- About 130 million years ago, plants "learned" to produce flowers in order to entice pollinators.

- As a result of an evolutionary adaptation to help them grasp tree branches, koalas have two thumbs on each hand.

- Before the creation of the first soils, early plants had to evolve means of surviving without it.

- Despite having a mole-like name, the Golden mole actually has shrew-like ancestry.

- The rapid eye movement (REM) sleep phase, when dreaming occurs, might have evolved to simulate threats and practice responses.

- Platypuses, which lay eggs, are one of the rare mammals that represent a primitive evolutionary branch.

- Because they consumed a lot of tough plants, our ancestors developed the appendix, which aids in the digestion of cellulose - an organ rarely used by humans today.

- In 1938, a species of fish once thought extinct—the "living fossil" coelacanth—was rediscovered in the wild.

- The "thumb" of the giant panda is actually an evolved wrist bone rather than a true thumb.

- The only surviving member of a once-diverse family of human species is Homo sapiens.

- The loss of vitamin C synthesis in primates, including humans, might be due to our fruit-rich ancestral diet.

- Arctic fish have evolved antifreeze proteins to stop ice crystals from forming in their blood.

- The emperor penguin, which is the largest species of penguin, is 4 feet tall, but earlier penguins may have been even taller.

- To elude predators, the mimic octopus can assume the appearance of up to 15 different marine species.

- Although modern birds are toothless, dinosaurs had teeth.

- Around 1.5 million years ago, Homo erectus may have used fire and sophisticated tools.

- The "waggle dance" of honeybees is an adapted way for them to communicate the location of food sources.

- Complex multicellular life was made possible by the evolution of the eukaryotic cell, which has a nucleus.

- Around 55-66 million years ago, grasses changed the landscape and paved the way for the emergence of animals that eat grass.

- Some animals, like the axolotl, display "neoteny," continuing to have juvenile characteristics as adults.

- Through convergent evolution, a marsupial known as the thylacine, also known as the Tasmanian tiger, came to resemble wolves.

- It is possible that cows have evolved social behavior because they have close friendships and get anxious when separated.

- An important development in the history of vertebrates was the evolution of the jaw in early fish.

- The largest bird in the world, the ostrich, descended from a smaller, flying ancestor.

- A reptile from New Zealand known as the tuatara is referred to as a "living fossil" because it has not changed much in 200 million years.

- Little leg spurs on some modern snakes, like boas and pythons, are left over from their ancestors who had legs.

- Walking on two legs, or bipedalism, evolved in humans before a large brain did.

- The flat fish called a flounder has an eye on each side when it is young, but as it gets older, one eye migrates.

- Many of the world's languages use a form of the word "mama" for mother, possibly due to the simplicity of lip formation in early human development.

- Populations that domesticated cattle and ingested milk past infancy experienced the evolution of lactose tolerance.

- The only mammal that solely consumes blood, the vampire bat, has developed specialized heat sensors to locate blood vessels.

- The eyes of the Mantis shrimp are ten times more color-sensitive than those of a human, including in ultraviolet light.

- Venom has evolved in some animals, including snakes and spiders, for a variety of reasons, including defense and predation.

- Native to the Americas, cacti evolved with spines in place of leaves to store water.

- In order to attract male bees for pollination, some flowers, like the bee orchid, have evolved to resemble female bees.

- Despite the giraffe's long neck, humans and giraffes both have seven neck vertebrae because of a common ancestor.

- From ants to elephants, social behaviors have evolved for a variety of reasons, including resource sharing and predator defense.

- The "Irish elk," which was neither unique to Ireland nor an elk, had antlers that could grow up to 12 feet long, the longest of any known deer.

- One of our closest relatives, the bonobo, communicates with a variety of vocalizations and gestures, displaying a complex social evolution.

- Archaeopteryx, the oldest bird ever discovered, lived about 150 million years ago and possessed both feathers and dinosaur-like characteristics.

- Sharks are older than trees in evolutionary terms.

- To avoid predators, some lizards have developed the ability to break off their tails, which they can then grow back.

Conclusion: Nature's Unending Story

In our remarkable journey through the annals of nature, we have delved deep into oceans brimming with intrigue, wandered through amazing forests, climbed the evolutionary ladders of untold species, and paused to reflect on the mysteries that still elude even the sharpest minds. Nature, with its awe-inspiring vastness, continuously surprises, enlightens, and captivates. As we reach the end of this curated collection of wonders, my aspiration is not just that you have amassed new knowledge, but that your admiration for our planet's infinite beauty and sophistication has deepened.

Each fact you have encountered here, regardless of its brevity or seeming inconsequence, represents a moment in a story that spans billions of years, underscoring nature's tenacity, creativity, and sheer brilliance. And within this expansive narrative of natural history, it is humbling to realize that the chapter of humanity is but a few pages. This perspective serves as a poignant reminder of our dual role as guardians of this world and as eternal learners, ever eager to explore and understand.

Your company on this exploration has been an honor. If this compendium of nature's tales has resonated with you, if you have found yourself marveling at a new discovery or revisiting a cherished known fact with fresh eyes, I would be truly appreciative if you would consider leaving a review. Your feedback not only helps others find and enjoy this journey but also fuels future quests into the captivating world of nature.

With hopes that your innate curiosity remains ignited and your sense of wonder ever vibrant, remember that though our book journey concludes here, nature's tales are ceaseless. Every dawn heralds new stories, enigmas, and splendors awaiting your discovery.

Until we meet again on another enlightening adventure,

-   *Dexter Informa.*

Preview of Dexter Informa's Interesting Facts About America

Early America

- The Poverty Point in Louisiana is considered the oldest known civilization in North America, dating back to 1650 BC.

- Some Vikings likely reached North America around the year 1000, 500 years before Columbus.

- Benjamin Franklin was not only a statesman but also an accomplished musician who played several instruments.

- Thomas Jefferson and John Adams both died on July 4, 1826, exactly 50 years after the signing of the Declaration of Independence.

- The American buffalo was not a buffalo at all; it is a bison.

- George Washington's teeth were not made of wood but rather a combination of gold, ivory, lead, and human and animal teeth.

- One of the first submarines was used during the Revolutionary War; it was called the Turtle.

- Harvard, established in 1636, is the oldest institution of higher education in the U.S.

- The first capital of the U.S. was not Washington D.C., but Philadelphia.

- Only one signatory of the Declaration of Independence was born in America: Edward Rutledge.

- The New Jersey campaign during the Revolutionary War witnessed more battles than any other state.

- Native American sign language was one of the most comprehensive sign languages ever developed.

- The shortest war involving American troops was in 1898 against Spain at Manila Bay, lasting only seven hours.

- The U.S. purchased Alaska from Russia for just $7.2 million in 1867.

- The Great Appalachian Valley played a major role in the westward expansion of early America.

- The first African American to formally practice medicine: James Derham, who did not hold an M.D. degree.

- In the 1700s, many believed tomatoes were poisonous.

- The original United States consisted of only 13 colonies.

- The dollar was adopted as the official monetary unit of the U.S. in 1785.

- Witches were hanged, not burned, during the Salem witch

trials.

- During the Revolutionary War, more soldiers died from disease than from combat.

- Paul Revere never shouted "The British are coming!" during his midnight ride.

- Native Americans used controlled fires to shape the Eastern U.S.'s landscape.

- The Boston Tea Party was not a party, and participants were disguised as Native Americans.

- The first person to walk across Niagara Falls on a tightrope was Charles Blondin in 1859.

- The original Pledge of Allegiance did not include the words "under God."

- Delaware was the first state to ratify the U.S. Constitution in 1787.

- The Liberty Bell was last rung on George Washington's birthday in 1846.

- The American Pyramid Mound City in Illinois contains over 120 earthen mounds.

- Martha Washington was the first woman to appear on a U.S. currency note.

- John Adams was the first to reside in the White House.

- The U.S. nearly went to war with Britain over a pig in the San

Juan Islands standoff in 1859.

- Native Americans introduced settlers to popcorn.

- The Mayflower Compact, signed in 1620, was the first governing document of Plymouth Colony.

- The Pony Express mail service lasted just 18 months from April 1860 to October 1861.

- The original game of "baseball" was brought to North America by British immigrants.

- The tallest President was Abraham Lincoln at 6'4".

- The U.S. Army was once smaller than the Army of Liechtenstein.

- Benjamin Franklin wrote a satire about farting called "Fart Proudly."

- Betsy Ross is widely credited with designing the first American flag, but there is no historical evidence to support this.

- The Mason-Dixon Line was a boundary dispute settled by astronomers.

- The State of Franklin once existed between North Carolina and the Mississippi River.

- St. Augustine, Florida, is the oldest continuously inhabited European-established settlement in the continental U.S.

- The most spoken language in the U.S. until the late 19th century was German.

- The United States doubled its land area with the Louisiana Purchase in 1803.

- In 1789, King Louis XVI gifted a key to the Bastille to George Washington. It is still on display at Mount Vernon.

- The first U.S. census in 1790 recorded a population of just under 4 million people.

- The Continental Congress declared the name of the new nation to be the "United States" of America, not just America.

- The Great Molasses Flood in Boston in 1919 killed 21 people.

- The U.S. state with the most battlefields preserved as national parks is Virginia.

- Geronimo was a famous Native American leader who fought against Mexico and the U.S.

- The first U.S. patent was issued in 1790 to Samuel Hopkins for a method of making potash.

- In the early 19th century, taking a bath in the winter was believed to be unhealthy.

- The first capital of the United States was New York City. In 1790, it moved to Philadelphia before settling in Washington, D.C.

- The U.S. Constitution was written on hemp paper.

- The first ambulance corps was developed during the Civil War.

- The term "Uncle Sam" was derived from Samuel Wilson, a meat packer from New York.

- The longest-serving member of the U.S. Congress was John Dingell, serving from 1955 to 2015.

- "Hail to the Chief" was not officially the Presidential Anthem until the 20th century.

- The U.S. Naval Academy in Annapolis was founded in 1845.

- One of the reasons the U.S. capital was moved from New York to Washington, D.C., was a deal over Revolutionary War debt.

- In the 18th century, lobster was so plentiful it was fed to prisoners and servants.

- During the Revolutionary War, one-third of the population was estimated to support the British.

- The U.S. faced a massive smallpox epidemic during the Revolutionary War.

- The 1800s Gold Rush was not limited to California. There were significant gold rushes in Georgia, North Carolina, and Alaska.

Check Out Dexter Informa's Other Interesting Facts Books

All these are available to buy on Amazon in both Kindle and paperback format

- Dexter Informa's Interesting Facts About America

If the links do not work, for whatever reason, you can search for these titles on the Amazon website to find them.